TEN
LITTLE
ELVES

Sandy Creek
NEW YORK

For Emily - our own little Christmas Elf
M.B.

For Erin & Isla
S.R.

An Imprint of Sterling Publishing
1166 Avenue of the Americas
New York, NY 10036

Text © 2016 by Mike Brownlow
Illustrations © 2016 by Simon Rickerty

ISBN 978-1-4351-6404-8

Manufactured in China
Lot #:
2 4 6 8 10 9 7 5 3 1
08/16

www.sterlingpublishing.com

TEN LITTLE ELVES

MIKE BROWNLOW SIMON RICKERTY

Ten little Christmas elves

are making toys until . . .

. . . Santa shouts, "The reindeer!

HELP!

I think they're really ill!

We need the magic cough drops from the Reindeer Doctor's cave.

Can you fetch them, little elves? Then Christmas will be saved!"

Ten little Christmas elves

think they've found a sign.

Now there are . . .

10

"WOOF!"

goes the husky team.

. . . nine.

Nine little Christmas elves,
getting in a state.

9

"WHAAAAH!"

Snowballs everywhere!

Now there are . . .

. . . eight.

**Eight little Christmas elves,
gazing up to heaven.**

8

"GRRRR!"

growls a polar bear.

Now there are . . .

. . . seven.

Seven little Christmas elves in a silly fix.

7

"YOO-EE-OOO!"

a yeti yowls.

Now there are . . .

. . . **six.**

**Six little Christmas elves
make a desperate dive.**

6

BRRRRR!

blows the icy storm.

Now there are . . . .

...five.

Five little Christmas elves
stand in shock and awe!

5

"WAH-HA-HA!"

the Ice Queen laughs.

Now there are . . .

...four.

4

Four little Christmas elves rest near Jack Frost's tree.

. . . three.

Three little Christmas elves find the Doctor's! Phew!

3

WHOOMF!

goes a fall of snow.

Now there are . . .

. . . **two.**

Two little Christmas elves,
on the homeward run.

2

CRACK!

goes the splitting ice.

Now there's only . . .

...one.

One little Christmas elf,
trudging through the snow,

1

Nearly out of energy,
what's that distant glow?

It's Santa's Grotto!

HIP HOORAY!

Her efforts weren't in vain.

The reindeer munch the cough drops
—now they all feel fine again!

They load the sleigh,
then **1, 2, 3**
and **UP** into the air,

Soon they'll be delivering
their presents everywhere!

High above the silvery clouds
the elf and Santa climb.

But they'll be back before too long and then it's

party time!

"Congratulations little elves!
You've just saved Christmas Day!"

Ten little Christmas elves all say,

"YAY!"

MERRY CHRISTMAS